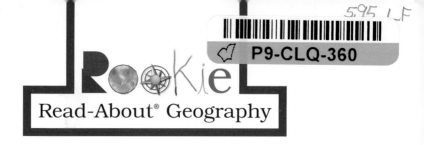

Alabama

By Holli Leber

Consultant
Nanci R. Vargus, Ed.D.
Assistant Professor of Literacy
University of Indianapolis
Indianapolis, Indiana

Children's Press®
A Division of Scholastic Inc.
New York   Toronto   London   Auckland   Sydney
Mexico City   New Delhi   Hong Kong
Danbury, Connecticut

Designer: Herman Adler Design
Photo Researcher: Caroline Anderson
The photo on the cover shows Bellingrath Gardens and Home in
Theodore, Alabama.

Library of Congress Cataloging-in-Publication Data

Leber, Holli.
  Alabama / by Holli Leber.
      p. cm. — (Rookie read-about geography)
Includes index.
Summary: A simple introduction to Alabama, focusing on its regions and
their geographical features.
  ISBN 0-516-22719-X (lib. bdg.)   0-516-27945-9 (pbk.)
  1. Alabama—Juvenile literature. 2. Alabama—Geography—Juvenile
literature. [1. Alabama.] I. Title. II. Series.
  F326.3.L43 2004
  917.6'1—dc22
                                              2003016891

Do you know why Alabama
is called the Heart of Dixie?

Dixie is a nickname for
the southeastern part of the
United States.

Alabama is right at the heart,
or middle, of this part.

Can you find Alabama on
this map?

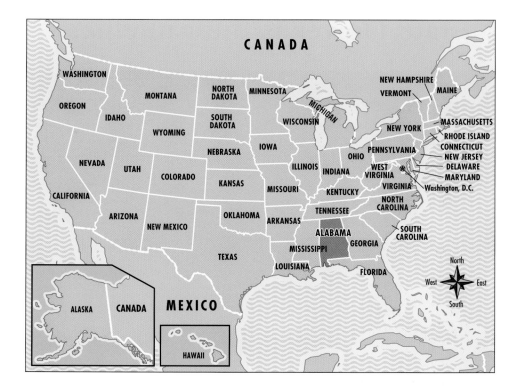

CANADA

WASHINGTON

OREGON

MONTANA

IDAHO

NORTH DAKOTA

MINNESOTA

NEW HAMPSHIRE

VERMONT

MAINE

WYOMING

SOUTH DAKOTA

WISCONSIN

MICHIGAN

NEW YORK

MASSACHUSETTS

RHODE ISLAND

CONNECTICUT

NEVADA

UTAH

COLORADO

NEBRASKA

IOWA

ILLINOIS

INDIANA

OHIO

PENNSYLVANIA

NEW JERSEY

WEST VIRGINIA

DELAWARE

MARYLAND

CALIFORNIA

KANSAS

MISSOURI

KENTUCKY

VIRGINIA

Washington, D.C.

ARIZONA

NEW MEXICO

OKLAHOMA

ARKANSAS

TENNESSEE

NORTH CAROLINA

SOUTH CAROLINA

TEXAS

ALABAMA

MISSISSIPPI

GEORGIA

LOUISIANA

FLORIDA

North

West

East

South

ALASKA

CANADA

MEXICO

HAWAII

5

In Alabama, shrubs and trees bloom in the spring. The state flower is the camellia.

The state bird is the yellowhammer.

There are mountains
and streams in northern
Alabama. The land is hilly
and covered with forests.

The soil is red because
it has iron in it.

Part of northern Alabama is called the Appalachian Highlands.

Coal, limestone, and marble can be found under the hills there.

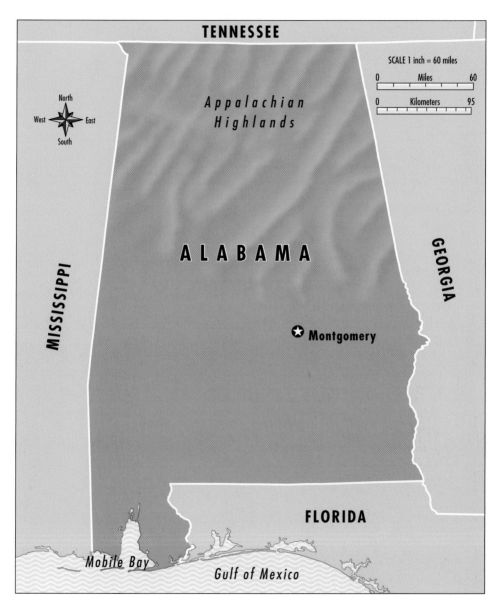

TENNESSEE

North
West ✦ East
South

SCALE 1 inch = 60 miles

0	Miles	60

0	Kilometers	95

*Appalachian
Highlands*

ALABAMA

MISSISSIPPI

GEORGIA

★ **Montgomery**

FLORIDA

Mobile Bay

Gulf of Mexico

11

The Piedmonts are south of the Highlands. These low hills are covered with trees.

Cheaha Mountain is the highest spot in Alabama.

The Black Belt crosses
the middle of Alabama.
This strip of land is named
for its sticky black soil.

In the past, cotton was
the main crop in Alabama.
It was grown in the
Black Belt.

Cattle

Farmers still grow cotton in the Black Belt. They grow corn, peanuts, and soybeans, too.

They also raise cattle, chickens, and hogs.

Pine forests cover part of
the Gulf Coastal Plain.
A plain is flat land.

The state tree is the
longleaf pine.

The rest of the Gulf Coastal Plain has swamps. A swamp is wet, spongy land.

Alligators and other animals live in the swamps.

The southern tip of Alabama is shaped like a boot heel. The heel is split in two by Mobile Bay.

Fishing and shipping are important jobs in this part of Alabama.

Birmingham is the largest city in Alabama. More steel comes from Birmingham than any other city in the South.

Capitol building in Montgomery

Montgomery is the state capital.

Huntsville is another large city in Alabama. The U.S. Space and Rocket Center is there.

Children visit the center
to learn what it is like to
be an astronaut.

Maybe you will visit
Alabama one day.

What part would you
most like to see?

Words You Know

alligator

camellia

Cheaha Mountain

cotton

longleaf pine tree

steel

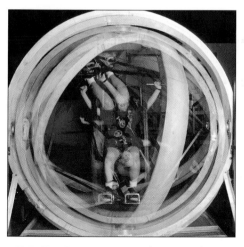

U.S. Space and Rocket
Center

yellowhammer

Index

About the Author

Holli Leber is a freelance writer. She has a Bachelor of Arts degree from Skidmore College. She lives in Saratoga Springs, New York.

Photo Credits

Photographs © 2004: Corbis Images/Bill Varie: 9; Dembinsky Photo Assoc.: 19, 20, 30 top left, 31 top left (Bill Lea), 6, 30 top right (Richard Shiell); ImageState/Andre Jenny: 25; Milton Fullman: 12, 15, 23, 30 bottom right, 30 bottom left; The Image Works: 26, 27, 31 bottom left (Michael J. Doolittle), 24, 31 top right (Karim Shamsi-Basha); Unicorn Stock Photos: 7, 31 bottom right (Robert E. Barber), 16 (Jeff Greenberg), 3 (Chuck Schmeiser), 8 (Dennis Thompson); William H. Allen: cover, 29.

Maps by Bob Italiano